PAPERS

Stories by
Undocumented Youth

Papers: Stories by Undocumented Youth

First Edition

Copyright © 2012 by Graham Street Productions, LLC
All rights reserved. Published in the United States by
Graham Street Productions

Graham Street Productions, LLC
1631 NE Broadway, #453
Portland, OR 97232

503-282-8683

For more information on the *Papers* documentary film or book,
please visit: http://www.papersthemovie.com

Printed in the USA with union labor

ISBN: 978-0-9857485-0-0

For more information on how to obtain an educational
license for the documentary film *Papers* or for bulk orders
of this book, please contact Graham Street Productions.

TABLE OF CONTENTS

T he *Papers* project began in 2007 in Portland, Oregon. Two teenagers, Cesar and Jose Luis, along with Rebecca, an adult mentor, created a three-minute video clip about coming of age as undocumented youth. The youth distributed the video clip widely and soon realized that there was huge interest in the issue of immigration generally, but more specifically in the problems undocumented youth face in the United States once they turn eighteen. Many people did not know about the issue and were amazed at what happens to youth who grow up in this country most of their lives, but find themselves hitting a brick wall when they graduate from high school. Because of this interest, a group of us, youth and adults, decided to make the documentary film *Papers: Stories of Undocumented Youth.*

Approximately two million undocumented children live in the United States, two million talented and able young people. Sixty-five thousand undocumented youth graduate from high school every year in the United States without "papers." In most states, they can't get a driver's license or state ID and in most cases it is against the law to work. It is difficult, if not impossible in some states, to attend college. Colleges and universities have varying policies about whether they accept undocumented students. If they are accepted, undocumented students are not eligible for federal financial aid. At the time of this writing, thirteen states provide undocumented students who have grown up in their states with the privilege of paying in-state tuition. In the other 37 states, an undocumented student must pay out-of-state or foreign student tuition which is much higher. Youth face these obstacles because of the decision of their families to immigrate, a decision that they had no say in. Their families just wanted safety, food, shelter or a better future for their children. I became involved in the *Papers* documentary film project from the beginning because I have friends and family who are undocumented and don't have the same rights as others who were born here. I thought that by participating in this project and helping to make a change, I would be able to help not just the people I know, but also thousands of other youth who deserve a shot at achieving their hopes and dreams. I also liked that I could work with my friends on the *Papers* Youth Crew and learn a lot of new skills for my future. Cesar, Jose Luis and I were the three original Youth Producers on the film crew. We called ourselves *El Grupo Juvenil.*

The *Papers* documentary film focuses on five individuals, their dreams, their challenges and the role of "papers" in their lives. Juan Carlos and Jorge are Mexican-American, Monica is Guatemalan-American, Yo Sub is Korean-American and Simone is Jamaican-American. These young people form the backbone of the film. Interviews with members of Congress, immigration leaders, faith leaders and individuals from around the country add to their stories. This issue affects people of all ages.

We released the film in September of 2009 and within a year it was shown to audiences in all 50 states, at the US Capitol and on hundreds of high school and college campuses. We continue to distribute the film to high schools, colleges, congregations and organizations across the country. I had hoped we would complete this film before the immigration reform debate heated up in Congress in 2010 and I am glad we did. I wanted people to become aware of what happens to the youth in their communities. I wanted this film to show that this issue affects millions of families who desire justice and work hard towards the dreams they want to accomplish here in the United States.

Many people who came to our house parties and events or followed us on Facebook and Twitter wanted to contribute to the film by donating money, by volunteering or by sharing their stories and skills. Fourteen hundred donors from 22 states donated to the *Papers* project. These donations made the film possible. So many youth wanted to participate that the original youth leaders opened up *El Grupo Juvenil* (the *Papers* Youth Crew) to all youth who wanted to help in some way. Over one thousand young people from across the country have participated in the production and distribution of the film.

Papers the Book grew out of the movie project. In 2009, the Youth Planning Program of the Vision into Action Coalition of the City of Portland, Oregon was offering grants to youth-led projects that were trying to fix an issue in the community. *El Grupo Juvenil* thought our issue was important to the community, so we wrote a grant proposal. A few months after applying we found out that we were awarded the grant. They liked what we were working on and what we were doing in the community. That grant gave us the seed funding for this book.

The producers of this film, including myself, talked to hundreds of students, many of them undocumented, from elementary school to college-age. Some live in fear every day about what could happen to them, about the chance that they will be arrested, detained and deported. Many students have a dream of going to a university, but for undocumented immigrants that's often not an option. Still, they want to tell their stories.

Young people from all over the country contacted us, wanting to share their stories. Some agreed to be filmed, others wrote their life story. There are so many youth with so many stories that need to be heard. The stories you will read here were written by students from across the country and range in age from ten to 32. They were eager to participate when they were told about the book. Some of the stories originally appeared on the DreamActivist.org website, an organization that has supported our work, and which, in such important ways, continues to work hard for the rights of undocumented youth.

As I read the stories that were submitted, I realized that Latinos are not the only undocumented immigrants living in the United

States. There are undocumented people from all over the world, and when reading their stories, I saw that they have suffered in many of the same ways, either in the countries they were born in, during the journey they undertook to get here or in their lives once they arrived. These are immigrants who can see a future here in the United States, not in the countries of their birth. This book, along with the film, will be distributed to middle schools, high schools and colleges around the country. We hope it will reach thousands of people who don't yet know about this issue or who know about it and want to make a difference. You can find out more about the *Papers* documentary film and book at www.papersthemovie.com.

We have worked hard to respect people's privacy, so we've allowed each writer to have an alias if they want one. This is designed to protect their identity and safety. Simply telling their stories increases the risk of being deported to a country they often can't remember.

Teachers helped us collect some of these stories. These teachers represent the many allies who helped with the project and help their own students every day. Teachers are sometimes in the best position to see the wall their students approach as they get close to graduating, the wall they hit when they walk across that stage. As we collected all the stories it was hard to decide which stories to pick since so many of them are worth hearing. We are so grateful to everyone who submitted their stories. We hope you enjoy and are inspired by the ones we chose for this first edition.

INTRODUCTION

Anne Galisky, *Papers* Documentary Film Director

ROMEO	What less than dooms-day is the prince's doom?
FRIAR LAURENCE	A gentler judgment vanish'd from his lips, Not body's death, but body's banishment.
ROMEO	Ha, banishment! be merciful, say 'death;' For exile hath more terror in his look, Much more than death: do not say 'banishment.'
FRIAR LAURENCE	Hence from Verona art thou banished: Be patient, for the world is broad and wide.
ROMEO	There is no world without Verona walls, But purgatory, torture, hell itself. Hence-banished is banish'd from the world, And world's exile is death: then banished, Is death mis-term'd: calling death banishment, Thou cutt'st my head off with a golden axe, And smilest upon the stroke that murders me.

— *Romeo and Juliet,* Act III, Scene III
by William Shakespeare
The Works of William Shakespeare,
The Globe Edition, 1862

For more than two million young people living in the United States without "papers," most brought here by their parents at an early age, the prospect of deportation looms large. Sometimes these youth only learn of their lack of legal status when the time comes to get a driver's license or apply for a first job, only to find out that they don't have a Social Security number. Even though these young people may feel American in every way, they have no path to citizenship and face what would more appropriately be called "banishment," being sent away from everything they know to a country that, for many, is completely foreign to them. The word "deportation" implies that there is somewhere to go back to; banishment is to be sent away into the wilderness.

Every year approximately 65,000 undocumented young people graduate from high school in the United States and find the door to their futures slammed shut. Many of them describe the experience as "hitting a brick wall." The writers of this collection came with families who emigrated from all over the world for many reasons, reasons no different from those of most Americans' ancestors since our nation's founding. We must remember that Native Americans whose forebears lived on this land for millennia and African Americans whose ancestors were forced into slavery have a different history in America. Immigrants have often come fleeing hunger, violence, poverty and tyranny to go towards opportunity, freedom and safety. The reasons for immigration have not changed but the rules have. Currently there is no path to citizenship for the vast majority of these young people. There is no "line" in which to get.

My dad, my aunts, my uncles and my grandparents were all once undocumented. I grew up hearing their immigration stories. They made it to the United States after a seven-year journey from the Ukraine via Mexico, arriving in 1935. They planned to come legally, worked hard and saved their money. But they were defrauded by an American attorney at the Juárez-El Paso border. He stole their hopes and their money. Eventually my grandfather hired *coyotes* to bring them across the Rio Grande.

My dad was four years old at the time, the youngest in the family. His older siblings remember riding across the river on horseback in the middle of the night. In the morning, my grandfather turned himself in to US Immigration authorities, thinking that if he could "just explain everything to the Americans," all would be put right. Instead, he was incarcerated and the whole family (my grandmother and the five children) were held under house arrest.

During the Red Scare of the 1950s, many immigrants from the Soviet Union were suspected of being communists and the family's immigration files were reopened. My father, who crossed the border with his parents and siblings when he was a very small child, was ordered deported to the country of his birth, Mexico. A few years ago, I asked my 78-year-old father a question I had somehow never thought to ask, "How did you feel during your deportation hearing?" When he answered, it was with great emotion and was one of the few times in my life I have ever seen him cry. He was alone when the Immigration hearings officer accused him of being disloyal to the United States. Soon after, my father received a notice of deportation in the mail. He panicked, not knowing what to do.

As my dad told this story, one I had heard my whole life, I finally had a clear view of him at age nineteen, bearing the crushing heartbreak of being rejected by his home, the only place he knew, his own country. I saw the hurt, many decades old. Ultimately, as it was the beginning of the Korean War, he was able to persuade the army to enlist him right away and so prove his loyalty. He was found to be "of good moral character" because he was willing to fight and die for the United States. This path to citizenship is not an option for undocumented people today.

In 2007, a small group of students and adult mentors, undocumented and documented, started work on a project that was to become a feature-length documentary film entitled *Papers: Stories of Undocumented Youth.* We thought that if we could bring to life some of the stories of undocumented young people we could persuade the American public to care about them and think about this complex situation in a more nuanced and compassionate manner. At that time, finding five people who were willing to take the risk of going public about their immigration status was a challenge. We started to collect written and recorded stories by undocumented youth, thinking that we might need actors or animation to portray their lives on film. Some of those stories are in this collection.

As we listened to these stories over the last five years, we have noticed the tone and content change. Several years ago, undocumented youth were much more isolated. Some of those who were the most "out" only knew each other by first names or aliases on social media. Now these activists have begun to deliberately use methods and language from the civil rights, women's rights and gay rights movements. In March 2010 in Chicago, DREAMers launched the first "Coming Out of the Shadows" event, organized by the Immigrant Youth Justice League, very much the superheroes that their name suggests. They call themselves DREAMers because they would be eligible for the DREAM Act, should Congress pass this legislation, which would provide some undocumented youth with a path to citizenship if they attend college or serve in the military and meet a series of strict requirements. Without the DREAM Act or some other immigration reform, there is no path to gain legal residence, no application to fill out, nothing in their control, nothing they can do to legalize their status. Even with the passage of the DREAM Act, a large number of young people will be ineligible.

These young activists have taken great risks and are part of a growing movement of undocumented youth who are no longer willing to hide in the shadows, organizing public "Coming Out of the Shadows" events across the country, marching on federal buildings and congressional offices, walking thousands of miles across the country to talk with other Americans, participating in hunger strikes, engaging in civil disobedience and carrying out sit-ins in congressional and campaign offices. They are even organizing from within Immigration and Customs Enforcement (ICE) detention centers to get their stories out and confront head-on the fear that has kept undocumented immigrants in the shadows for so long. The social activism and political organizing led by youth activists added to the pressure that brought the DREAM Act to a vote in 2010 and to President Obama's June 15, 2012 announcement of Deferred Action for Childhood Arrivals (DACA).

The liberation movement of DREAMers is centered on the telling of their stories. Everything that they do, from marches to sit-ins, from petition-gathering to hunger strikes, is to bring attention to their stories because they believe that if only they were known and understood by their neighbors, their request for legal inclusion into American society could not be denied.

Telling stories changes people, both the teller and the listener. Even as undocumented youth put themselves at risk by going public about their lives, I believe that the telling of their stories has lessened their depression and their isolation, brought them untold numbers of allies and gained the attention of Congress, the media, the American public and the President. The more seasoned undocumented activists among them have been insisting for several years that making yourself more public is actually safer in the long run. Telling the truth about who you are can be both dangerous and liberating. It is one of the most fundamentally human of activities. It is moving and intimate to read these stories and the barriers that we imagine between us fall away as we hear about these young people's lives in their own words.

Last summer I spoke with Hector Lopez, a college student from Milwaukie, Oregon who was deported to Mexico the year before at the age of nineteen. He had lived in the United States his entire life, ever since he was six weeks old. A former high school student body president and Little League coach, he didn't even know he was undocumented.

One day, as he walked from his parents' suburban house to his car to go to the gym, armed agents surrounded him shouting, "We're ICE and you are under arrest!" He responded, "What's ICE?!" literally not knowing anything about the agency (Immigration and Customs Enforcement), an encounter with which many undocumented immigrants live in daily fear.

Within days and without ever appearing before a judge, he was taken by plane from Seattle heading south. He did not know where he was going and no one would tell him. When he arrived late that night, he found out that he was in an Immigration facility in Brownsville, Texas. He waited in line to get processed and then was sent through a one-way turnstile across the Mexican border into the night. "All I had with me were the clothes I was wearing to go to the gym the day I was picked up: gym shorts, a sweatshirt, $30 in cash, my wallet, phone and car keys…They gave me a pack of ramen noodles, a water bottle, and some crackers."

"I don't even speak Spanish! I got a 'C' in Spanish! My parents didn't want me to have an accent; they wanted to assimilate and wanted us to assimilate even more. We didn't even eat Mexican food at home. We had meatloaf. I don't even know where the accent marks are supposed to go on my name!" Hector remarked to me.

Hector took a bus to Mexico City and finally met up with his father who was also deported. The first couple of days Hector's thoughts quickly went from, "I miss this, I'm gonna miss that" to "oh man, I'm gonna die."

Hector was targeted as an American by gang members. "They assumed I had money. They hung up an American flag across from where we lived. They chased me and I hid." Their neighbor's daughter was brutally murdered. He was scared and wouldn't leave the small apartment where they were staying. He lost twenty pounds. Hector became suicidal. "It's almost like you don't exist anymore, like you've gone into a black hole and are floating outside of the universe. You're there, but you're not real."

Hector decided to go back to the US border where he applied for asylum and was taken into custody by US Immigration authorities. He hopes that his story will help persuade a judge that he belongs here in the United States. "My life is here. I only have one home."

The banishment of so many of our young people into the desert of the unknown is the definition of scapegoating. They and their hard-working parents are heaped with all the blame of a poor economy, high unemployment and polarized politics and then driven out, sometimes literally, into the desert. As with scapegoating of any kind, even when driven out, the problems for which they are blamed are still with us. To banish them to countries unknown to them is both cruel and stupid. This reckless swinging at imagined foes is a plague on all our houses. They have everything to give to our country and want only to belong.

Here are their stories, thirty of two million.

– Anne Galisky
August 2012

ACT I

The Star Sacrifices Itself

My mom, out of desperation, brought me to this country. She left everything in Jamaica to come here, she sold whatever she had to come here. She didn't have any possessions back in Jamaica. She came here and she brought me here with her with the promise that she'd eventually figure something out, figure a way to get everything done. But she had no knowledge of the immigration system. She was ignorant to it. A few months after I came here, she became undocumented and so she became very afraid, afraid that if she went to Immigration and asked about it she would be detained, afraid that she couldn't trust anyone.

— Simone, *Papers* documentary film

My name is Eliseo. I am twelve years old and an eighth grader in middle school. I was brought to the United States by my parents when I was six years old. Unfortunately, the difference between me and other kids is that I'm undocumented. Most students are taught to dream and mold their future. I can see my future but I'm being told that I don't have one.

One of my favorite things to do is to go to the public library. I like to read and learn about astronomy. I love to get lost in the books. Did you know that our universe is always expanding and infinite at the same time? My dream is to go to college and get my degree in astronomy. When I learn and study about the universe I feel I will be able to passionately contribute knowledge back to my community.

I am excited to start high school next year. I want to explore my talents and find out what I'm best at. But my peers and I already feel like we don't have the support or a purpose to succeed in high school. Because of this divide some of my peers are going to make bad decisions. They are going to think that they don't have many options and not try. I don't want to become a statistic. I want to succeed. I want to do something good for my family. I want to graduate from high school, go to a university and graduate with a bachelor's degree. I want to have the skills to navigate an immigration system that is as complicated as our solar system. I don't want to deal with uncertainty about my future. I'd rather spend my energy dealing with the uncertainty of why our universe is heavy or what this dark matter is all about.

My parents are farmworkers. They wake up at 5:00 am every morning to go to work. Every day I go through the day never knowing whether they will come home or not. I live in fear and uncertainty, but I don't want to give up or lose hope. I want to become a full citizen of these United States. I want to be a positive role model. I want to do this for my parents, because to me my parents are like stars. Stars only live to be around ten billion years old. Before a star dies it crunches up into what is called a "red giant" then it explodes. But the star doesn't just die, its matter and gas helps create new stars. The star sacrifices itself to create new life, just like my parents are doing for me.

I am not asking for a handout. All I want is the opportunity to earn the things that I want, to make my dreams come true and to be able to give back to my community and this country, which I consider my own.

My name is Dan. I'm twenty years old and I currently live in Florida. I was born in Colombia and came to the US on a tourist visa at the age of eleven. At the time I thought I was just taking a vacation and visiting my relatives who had been living here legally for many years. My intention was to try and think about something other than the great tragedy I had suffered just two weeks before. It turns out that going back was not an option because there would be nobody there waiting for me. My father died two weeks before I came here and my mother died three years prior to that when I was eight. The only family I had left was my sister who is five years older than me. I needed someone to look after me and that someone was a permanent resident living here in the United States for many years. She was my aunt but she has now become a like a mother to me. Because of technicalities, I wasn't able to adjust my status and I am the only member of my family without legal status.

I am a part-time college student majoring in Finance and I have a 4.0 GPA. I wish I could go to school full-time but because Florida charges me as an out-of-state student, I have to pay close to $1000 per class at a community college. Therefore one or two classes is all I can afford. I've had to turn down scholarships and job offers due to my undocumented status.

I often find myself lying to my closest friends every time they ask me about my life. "Why don't you have a job, car, or even a license? How come you're not going to school full-time?" It's frustrating not being able to just let it all out but I'm afraid they won't understand since they've never had to go through what I'm going through right now.

I am not asking for a handout. All I want is the opportunity to earn the things that I want, to make my dreams come true and to be able to give back to my community and this country, which I consider my own.

My mother was never able to finish high school, so she never believed in herself. People would tell her that she was too poor because she wore old clothes passed down from her sister, and that she was an "illegal," so she dropped out of school.

My family emigrated from Mexico twenty years ago. My mom was only fifteen when she came. She told me it was a horrible experience. She came with her little brother, who was eight years old, and her best friend. They were the only two girls in a group of 25 crossing the border.

My mother was never able to finish high school so she never believed in herself. People would tell her that she was too poor because she wore old clothes passed down from her sister, and that she was an "illegal," so she dropped out of school.

I would like to be an architect when I grow up. I love drawing and math. I would love to design houses and buildings. We don't have a lot of money in my family, but my mother is pushing me to get an education because she was never able to. She's willing to do anything to help me graduate.

I came to the USA at the age of thirteen. My parents' plan was to finally reunite and save enough money to buy a house in Mexico. I saw it as an adventure, while my younger brother disagreed with the whole plan altogether. The promise was that we were going to be back in Mexico in less than two years. My dad had to come to the USA. I was thirteen and very sick; they needed money. He broke US immigration law to save my life.

Only my mother knew that we were going to be smuggled into the United States. My brother and I found out at the Mexico/USA border. It was pitch black when we ventured through the desert in Nogales into US territory. The smugglers were high on cocaine. They carried guns. They were lost and we had no choice but to follow. The coyotes howled without fear, each time closer to us. There were a lot of them: a dozen…a hundred…a thousand. I could not tell because I was too young and afraid to count the coyotes in the desert. The moon was as big as a fist. We got near a bunch of trees, near other people and other smugglers hiding in the rocks and the grass.

I could hear the sound of the Border Patrol nearby looking for me; a helicopter cut the darkness with a beam of pure white light. I knew at that moment that I was a criminal. I broke a law but I could not go back. I couldn't tell my mother to go back. The smugglers were going one direction which was north and we were in their hands until my father paid for our release. I was afraid of the police, of the smugglers, of the coyotes and of myself.

Unlike many DREAMers, I had always felt like a criminal. I was old enough to know that jumping the fence was not legal. My entry was not sanitized with a passport or a temporary visa. Still, I could do little about it. I cannot blame my parents either. Maybe it's my father's fault, but he lost a finger at work and they didn't even pay his medical bills. His hands are oily and rough from hard work. He lost his hand lines working for a third of what a logger earns. I told him that since he has no hand lines, he has no destiny. He is free to make his own. In a way, that is the reality of all immigrants in the US. We lost the destiny we had. We died on the border and someone else was born, someone without destiny.

When I went to high school someone told my mother to enroll me in the tenth grade. It was a mistake and I went to high school when I was supposed to enter the eighth grade. Still I graduated high school within the top 15% of my class with a 3.75 grade point average. I took a lot of English classes in college and finally graduated with a degree in Communication Design.

I am one class away from finishing an Economics degree. The dream of my life is to go to film school and to become either a movie director or a college professor. At times, I want to give up because it feels impossible. Then I remember how I came to this country: with only the clothes I was wearing, skinny, cold and covered with mud. How did I manage to get a college degree? I don't know because I am always broke and I do not feel especially bright or talented. One professor told me I "was dumb like a bag of hammers but…God can make five pounds of bread with one pound of flour!"

I know that I am better off being an "illegal alien" in the US than a citizen in any country in the world. Still, why do I have to give up my humanity? Why can someone else have the right to tell me what I am or am not? It is not their right to scream that this is not my country. It is a matter of belonging. I study hard to be a better person. I volunteered in a hospital and later worked to increase the wages of our local firefighters. I was paid less than half of what I was supposed to be paid to organize a community to clean its water.

It is time to call things by their name without anyone having the right to say it isn't so. This country does not belong to me. I belong to this country.

R ight now we are in the Court of Immigration with my mom. Two years ago, my mom got caught by Immigration in a raid at her work. When I found out about it, I couldn't hold it in, I burst into tears, I couldn't stop. We have to wait until they call her into the Court.

I was born in San Diego, California. I have four siblings – three brothers and one sister. My two older brothers were born in Mexico. My mom immigrated to the United States when she was very young. I don't exactly know how old she was, but she came when she was very young.

The day that the raid happened there was a school assembly where my sister and some of her classmates performed some dances. When the assembly ended I saw my aunty and cousin. She asked me if I knew what time my mom was getting out of work. I told her that I didn't know and she went to the school office. Then I went outside for a kickball tournament with my class against another fourth grade class. One of the teachers came outside and told me that my brother was there to pick me up from school.

When I got to the office I saw my sister crying and I asked her, "Why are you crying?" My sister told me that Immigration had our mom. I just burst into tears. My aunty told me and my sister that we had to go spend the night at her house. People were saying that Immigration was breaking into people's houses. We were scared, so we left with my aunty and went to her house.

We had also heard that Immigration was trying to get into my brothers' high school. I was scared because my brothers were at school. Twenty minutes later my older brother showed up at my aunty's house and asked how me and my sister were doing. I just covered my face with a pillow and started to cry because I was so sad I couldn't hold it in. I just needed to cry.

I calmed down a bit and I watched some movies with my cousin and then we went outside to play to distract ourselves. We went to the park across the street and played tag. Time passed and we had to go to bed. I was woken up in the middle of the night because my mom had been released and we could go home.

My mom struggles, but we are trying to help her however we can. It's pretty hard for us because we might have to go to Mexico for a very long time and I don't want that to happen. If we leave we would be leaving everybody who we have gotten to care about and love behind. They have gotten to love us too.

Now we have to wait until Court is over. We are going to be stuck here for more than two hours.

M y family comes from Cuernavaca, Mexico. My mom came to the United States when she was nineteen years old. My brother was born in Mexico. He was a few months old when my mother brought him to the United States. My father was already working here so that he could pay the *coyote* who would bring my mother and brother here. My mom made it to the United States but they suffered a lot on the way here. She didn't really eat. She would just take bites off of whatever they gave her to eat.

Once she arrived, my mom didn't know any English so she couldn't get a job. Anyway, my dad didn't let her have a job because of jealousy. He thought that if my mom worked she would leave him. Since my dad didn't know any English either, people would steal from him.

After a while my dad became a drug dealer. Eventually he got caught by the police and went to jail. After a few years he got deported.

Years went by. My mom suffered a lot to get us, my younger sister, my older brother and me, through life. She had to work two jobs in order for us to go to school. One of her dreams had been for us to be born in the United States. Her second dream is for us to go to college.

Ever since she told me about our family's past, I've felt so good knowing the truth, knowing that my mom didn't lie to me about my dad and what he has done.

After some years, my mom met my stepdad – his name is Carlos – and, with his help, she's gotten us through all the trouble that we've had. Thanks to him I can probably have my dream come true. My dream is to become a pediatrician someday.

Right now I'm just hoping to make my mom proud of me. My older brother has made her happy because he's in college now. I want to make her happy by giving her my diploma when I graduate from high school and go to college. That's my dream.

I am from Oaxaca, Mexico and I feel proud that I come from that country. I'm currently in high school and I'm a student with many dreams and someone who hopes to make them a reality some day. I would like, one day, to become an excellent veterinarian, and be of service to my community through that, and to animals, of course. I will tell you a little bit about my story and how difficult it still is for me, as a laborer before and now as a student fighting for what he wants.

I come from a family of eight children, four boys and four girls. Our family is low-income and our parents have always wanted the best for us. They have done everything they could to put food on the table every day. All of my brothers and sisters went to school, but were not able to finish due to lack of money. The cruel poverty we lived in was such that there would be days that we would go without even a bite to eat, days that we would all go on an empty stomach. Some of my siblings went as far as elementary school, but after that they lost the hope of being able to continue with their education because it was so expensive.

I finished middle school just before turning fifteen years old, and I was clearly eager to move forward. That's where my pain started because my parents told me it would not be possible for me to continue with my education due to lack of money. Believe me that was a hard blow for me.

After that happened, I decided I would come to this country so I could work hard and give a better life to my family. When the day finally came for me to set out and leave my roots behind, it was all very hard because I was only fourteen years old. The whole route to get to the border was difficult. We had to go through much suffering, the likes of which I never imagined. When we reached the border I was afraid, very afraid. I was having never-ending feelings and thoughts going through my head such as, "what and how would my life be from this moment on?" I felt happy, but I felt sad at the same time because I was afraid to encounter a new world and new country.

I've suffered a lot to be here, from being put in a trunk so that the cops wouldn't see us, to having bad people treat us like criminals with no mercy. Once I arrived, I immediately began to work in the fields picking grapes and enduring the immense heat that would beat down on us every day. It was really hard work. I never imagined that the US would be like that, but it was, it was. I worked more than you can imagine. This was back when I was fifteen years old. You can imagine how difficult it was and the headache I would get from thinking I had missed the opportunity to get a better education. Thanks to those hard knocks I began to value life and to enjoy and love everything I had. I gained a greater appreciation for my family and began to feel proud of them.

One day a friend of mine invited me to a party in another state and I accepted so I could see my sister who I had not seen for over five years. The party would only be for one day, but I accepted just the same. I got to the party and went to see my sister. It was all so beautiful. We went to the party, enjoyed ourselves, and had a good time, that is, until the party ended. It was so sad. I went to say goodbye to my sister that same night. I felt bad because I didn't know how much time would pass before we saw each other again. But she surprised me with something that would change my life completely. She offered to have me stay with her. Yes, with her! The nicest thing about it was that she asked me to stay and enroll in school to continue with my education. Honestly, I was confused. It all happened so quickly.

Without thinking twice, I accepted her offer. I thought of the great sense of fulfillment I would get from returning to school thanks to my brother-in-law and my sister, who I love and to whom I will be forever grateful. I am now in my senior year of high school. I had to go through many hardships because of not knowing how to speak English, and not knowing how the school system works, but I've kept moving forward. I'm doing my best. There are certainly good times just like there are bad ones. I feel really happy and grateful that life has given me another opportunity to start over.

I ask you all through this simple letter to support us. I ask that you grant us the same opportunities and that you allow us to achieve our goals. I fear that tomorrow I may be unable to continue with my education and begin my career. I hope our voice is heard. This was just some of my story, and there are many others just like me.

Translated from Spanish by Héctor M. Miramontes

ACT II

The Brick Wall That Never Crumbles

I think everybody has it hard. Everyone has to struggle to get where they want to be. I don't think there's a person that ever had it really easy to get where they wanted to be. My big struggle right now is not having the documents to do pretty much everything. I can't drive. I can't have an ID. I can't have a job. Just because of the papers. It makes it hard. It makes it a little hard to go through life everyday.

— Juan Carlos, *Papers* documentary film

he brick wall that never crumbles, the brick wall that we hit every time we believe a door has been opened for us. The uncertainty of a successful future. The exhaustion of always maintaining hope and being let down. The exhaustion of maintaining the thought of things turning out well in the end. The feeling of detachment from the rest. The idea of knowing that everyone around us is headed for success while we are stuck in the middle of everything, always moving backwards, never moving forward. Nowhere to run. Where do we stand? What about us? Does anyone care? Do we deserve this? At times we want to scream to the world and tell them that we cannot do this anymore, that we are scared, that we need guidance, that it is not easy. All we want is to find the light because we can no longer stay in this tunnel, hitting that brick wall every time we believe we see the end of the tunnel.

All we really want is to fulfill our dreams. Isn't that what everyone wants? So why can't we fulfill ours? Not having papers does not define who we are, it simply limits us. It doesn't tell of our success, it doesn't tell of our story, it doesn't show our hard work. We spend our lives working extremely hard, making ourselves and our loved ones proud and later realize that we have nothing to look forward to once high school is over, or once we turn eighteen. So where do we go from here? Only time will tell. Until then we will remain determined to achieve our goals, hopeful that one day we will have the opportunity to do so.

I feel like my hands are tied behind my back and I feel unable to take control of my future. I came to this country when I was eleven from Colombia. At first, the fact that I was undocumented didn't really mean that much to me. But as I grew up and understood the reality of the situation I was in, my dreams were shattered. My parents gave up so much for my brother and me to get to where we are now. And now that I'm about to graduate from high school with a 3.8 GPA and various extracurricular and community activities, I feel that all the hard work and interest that I put in the past years was for nothing.

For every job, scholarship or other program that I have applied to, I fulfill all their requirements except the "Must be a US Citizen" one. And every time I read those words, it just breaks my heart and my dreams to know that I'm simply not allowed to dream and have goals. Even when many doors are closed, I try to remain hopeful that one day I'll be able to go into medicine and help others. But in this situation I do not know what to expect anymore. My only hope is that President Obama gives us this opportunity. We need the DREAM Act to pass.

Even when many doors are closed,
I try to remain hopeful that
one day I'll be able to go into
medicine and help others.

I was one of those US citizens who didn't really know what having "papers" meant until I saw what happened to a good friend of mine who didn't have them.

For immigrants, "papers" are an important thing to have if you live in the United States. But some US citizens who have papers don't really know how much power those papers have.

I was one of those US citizens who didn't really know what having papers meant until I saw what happened to a good friend of mine who didn't have them.

It was a nice day. I went to work at 10:00 a.m. I know everyone says that fast food restaurants are a bad place to work, but I loved to go to work. To this day I think it was the best job I've ever had. My friend was one of the cooks. I've known her for about eight years. She doesn't have papers and she's been in this country for ten years. She has worked at this fast food restaurant for five years and never had problems until the labor inspectors came. They wanted to know if everyone working there had the right documents to be working there. If not, they had to voluntarily leave or the manager would have to pay a large fine.

The managers refused to pay so she had to leave or else Immigration would be called. The bad part was that she had to quit that same day. She was seven months pregnant. She started crying because her husband had just lost his job as well.

I felt really bad because I didn't need the job as much as she did. I was willing to quit my job so that she could keep hers. The manager said he couldn't do it.

That day I finally realized that people who don't have papers really need them because they can't have a job, students can't keep going to school and at any time they can get deported. Now I appreciate the fact that my whole family has residency because I don't have to live with the fear of them being forced to leave me.

I am an undocumented youth. I was nine months old when I came to the United States. I was born in Mexico, but I was raised in the United States. I have seven sisters and one brother. There are so many things that I remember from when I was little. I remember my mom and dad didn't have much money to buy food after paying the rent. I was just happy to have a place to live.

My older sister, Elisabeth, was the first in my family to finish high school. She was the sister I looked up to because she showed me that I could finish high school too. Because our two older sisters got pregnant and dropped out of high school, Elisabeth decided to graduate to set a better example for her younger sisters.

Elisabeth was my sister, friend and role model. She was like a mom to me. The day I found out that she had died it was hard for me to think of anyone else I could look up to. Four years ago she passed away and it is still hard for me to know that she is not here. Someone took my sister and I can't get her back. I made a promise to her that I was going to finish high school and now I'm the second one to finish high school and the first one to go to college. It feels so good to know that I reached my goal.

I have so many dreams. One is to finish college and from there go to law school. But it's hard for me to go to college because I don't have papers. I can't get financial aid.

I'm eighteen years old. I was raised in the USA. This is my home. Here I have a home and a school and dreams to accomplish. I'm in college now and my hope is to be able to finish. From there I would go to law school and make my dreams come true.

Those are my dreams, and my dreams are the same as anyone else's. But there are some things that get in my way. I do not have legal status. My hope is to make my family proud.

Since I was little, I have worked at many jobs. I helped my parents sell Mexican bread in the streets. I helped them pick up and sell wood pallets so my family could make money when we were going through some hard times. I also delivered newspapers to get my family some money. My brothers and I sold ice cream to gather money for our school supplies and clothes for school.

To be a youth these days is hard because of the gangs and violence in the streets. Many families don't have enough money. They need to move often and do not have enough food to eat and can barely buy clothes because of the economics of their family.

In America we have a problem with gangs. Some say that people join a gang because they are undocumented, that because of their immigrant status and the problems it causes, they get involved with gang life. In my opinion, a person who wants to join a gang will, no matter what their immigrant status. But I also think that it is less likely for an undocumented person to join a gang because they know that if they get in trouble with the law it is more likely that they will be deported. They won't risk getting caught and deported just to be in a gang.

They would do what most other undocumented immigrants come here for: work and support their families, set down roots for their kids and make sure there is enough food on the table. That's what an undocumented person comes to do in America – to have a better life than the one they had before, to see their kids be better educated and succeed in life, to see that their kids don't have to work ten hours a day breaking their backs just to support their families.

An undocumented person comes to America to have the American Dream but without documents it is very hard for them.

I am undocumented, unafraid, unapologetic and I come from a background of privilege. Unlike many undocumented youth, when I went to the DMV (Department of Motor Vehicles), I walked out with a license.

My driver's license has always been my passport to this society. It has allowed me to remain in denial about my status and have some level of normalcy. It made hiding in the shadows so much easier and I still can't believe I got it.

When my family and I emigrated from Jordan to Chicago in 1993, escaping an impoverished economy, my father knew very well that we were on a tourist visa that was sure to expire. I was six and my brother was two. My Social Security card had written on it very clearly "Not Valid for Work." I remember thinking, "Well, I don't need to work." I must've been ten. I remember looking at it again when I was eighteen, desperately thinking, "How will I ever get a job?" But this number, though not valid, was so crucial to living well in the shadows. Lucky for me, that number was also on my ID.

When I turned fifteen, I took driver's education classes. I applied for the classes using that magical not-valid-for-work number. When I turned sixteen my dad and I went to the DMV. He was more scared and nervous than me. I was strangely calm. I went up to the lady behind the counter. She asked for my ID. I gave it to her. She jotted down some information and asked for my Social Security number. I pointed to my ID and told her that it was on there.

"But I need to see the actual card. Do you have it with you?"

"No, I forgot it at home," I lied. "But it's the same exact number." She looked at me from under her glasses.

"Oh no, honey, I need to see the card because I need to make sure it's the right number."

We went back and forth as I nervously tried to convince her that she had nothing to worry about; it was the right number. I was sure I would have to give up and go back to my home in the suburbs where you can't get anywhere without that passport to society: a driver's license. She paused for a second, looked at me, and asked, pointing at my hijab with her pen, "Do you always wear that?"

I was taken aback by the question but quickly answered, "No, I take it off when I'm home."

"Oh. Because I'm Jewish, you know, and some Orthodox Jewish women cover their hair like that too."

"You're Jewish?" I asked, relieved to get off the topic of my not-valid-for-work nine digit number. "I'm Muslim! Did you know both Jews and Muslims don't eat pork?!"

Thinking back about it, I laugh at my desperate attempt to draw some connection between us and to have her relate to me. I wanted her to see something of herself in me. You can't deny a person you relate to.

She was intrigued. We spoke a little about our religions, on some differences and similarities.

"Alright," she said finally, "Are you *sure* this is the right number?" pointing again to my ID.

"Yes."

"Okay. I'll let it go this time, but next time, I'll have to see the card."

And just like that, I had my license. That was it. My father couldn't believe I got it. I couldn't believe it either. I also couldn't believe how much power people behind the counter at the DMV have. It's incredible. I was so relieved she was able to relate to me on some level and that she saw a human and not just a number. The next day at school, I showed off my new license. I was normal again, if only temporarily.

The Undocumented

Tall, short, fat, skinny, thin
we see them every day
laughing, happy, crying, stressed, depressed
the undocumented...

Young, old, hard working
Carefree, careful, careless
fretful, gleeful, determined
the undocumented...

What right have they?
To "sponge" on the health care?
what right have they
to accept the cheapest jobs?
what right have they
to "invade"?

What right have they?
Except the human right
to be educated,
to work for their daily bread
to get a shot at their hopes and dreams

And if?

If they are innocent in being here
if they had no choice in getting on
that bus, boat, plane, train

If they had no idea
of the consequences
of following their parent

If they were too young
to make a legal or sound decision
Do they still
deserve to be called and classified as

the undocumented?

ACT III

For This, Sometimes I Cry

I told my teacher that we got this letter at home saying that Immigration wanted to see us. I told her that we were scared because even though the letter said they wouldn't take us into custody or anything, I told her that we were scared that they would. She started to cry and I started to cry and she didn't know what to do and she really, really wanted to help.

— Monica, *Papers* documentary film

My name is Eric, and I was brought up to the United States when I was ten months old.

When I was little and I started school in kindergarten, I remember everyone used to make fun of me because of how I looked, old clothes and messed up hair. As the years went by, I grew mad at the world because I was pushed to the point where I broke down and cried. No one ever said "leave him alone" or "that's enough." Everyone just kept laughing at me and every time that happened the teacher would take me out of class. I'd get sent to the office to tell the principal what happened, then they would explain the situation to my mom and by the time I was in fifth grade I got switched to a different school.

An undocumented youth is strong but also weak. Why? Because we work harder at our goals than documented youth do even after high school. But we are also weak because as undocumented people we realize that when we graduate we are not eligible for anything like work, college or driving. Some of us realize it before we graduate, like. I realized it when I was fourteen years old. This lowered my self-esteem just like any other undocumented youth's self-esteem would be lowered. Then we ask ourselves "why should I bother when there's no hope at all?" From that point everyone gets depressed and some people have thoughts of suicide because of the uselessness they feel they are to society. Why do they have those thoughts? Because of their immigration status. At least in my experience that's how I felt.

I am strong but I'm also weak. I'm strong because no matter how hard this crooked pathway is to follow I still don't give up. Why? Because there are things and people I care about. I've still got a lot to give, and most importantly because of my sweetheart who I would hate to see cry if I was gone. I'm weak too because I get overwhelmed with the stress, the depression, the madness, the sadness, the fact that I can't work, go to college, or drive which still really breaks me down. I hardly have any money and I can't get around anywhere especially to my girlfriend's house, and so all this hatred, anger, sadness, and stress make me feel like my own worst enemy. I feel I must get out of the darkness and go into the light. People need to take the time to read between the lines and realize

that we are all human. We are humans just trying to live our lives and provide for our families.

What bothers me about not being able to drive is that at times I spend a lot of time on the bus trying to get to places, especially to my girlfriend's house. It takes at least two-and-a-half hours to get to my girl's house. What makes me sad about this is that by not being able to drive I can't spend all the time I want with her. What makes me feel the worst about this is that I want to be the one who drives her to work, I want to be the one who picks her up at night when she comes out of work and I want to be the one who takes her out on dates in a car. It makes us both sad because we want to see each other and this barrier is in my way. When I'm alone I get mad and start to cry silently because of all these things in my way. I just wanna be with my girl and be happy with her. It makes me so miserable knowing I can hardly spend time with her. She gets sad too and she wants me there with her. Sometimes I don't know what's worse, not being with my sweetheart or not having papers. For this, sometimes I cry and get mad.

I came from Laos five years ago. I speak three languages: Lao, Thai, and English. I attend a bilingual Spanish-English school so I can learn to speak Spanish. The story that I'm going to tell you is not about me, but about a young man who has high hopes and dreams for his future. There are a lot of students among us who are undocumented. One of them is my best friend.

He wants to go to college and wants to work so that he can have a successful career. But he can't because he doesn't have papers. He's been here practically his whole life because he came to the United States from Mexico when he was two. I mean, you can't blame him for not having papers because his parents made a choice to get their son to the United States to get a better education.

I believe that someone who has been here that long should automatically get US citizenship. At this point he is basically an American. He grew up and adapted to this culture long ago, but because he doesn't have "papers," he can't be an "American." That one piece of the puzzle makes him incomplete. My best friend loves to play football and baseball. He always works hard at school. He never gets in any trouble. He wants to go to a university and major in Medicine.

Last summer my best friend's brother got into huge trouble that caused his whole family to be in an unimaginable situation. He got into a fight with someone who later told the police that there were weapons and drugs at my friend's house. At three in the morning the police busted the door open and used a stink bomb. They were pointing an M-4 assault rifle and shotguns at the back of a sixteen-year-old high school student awakened by the loud noise.

The police searched every single room in the house and found nothing. They couldn't find anything to support the accusations. Homeland Security took the whole family to jail. Now they are under probation and have to report every month to make sure that they can't escape.

I just can't believe that a thing like that is happening to my very closest friend. It hurts me to see it happening. The worst thing is that I can't do anything to help him. Now they are waiting for their court date so that a judge can set the date to send them back to Mexico. I really want to help but I don't know how the law is designed.

The day that I found out that I was undocumented was during my sophomore year. The room was very, very dark. I think it was September. It was raining. Both of my parents had just come out of work, so they were in their work clothes. My sister and I were like, "What's going on?"

Our parents started telling us everything about how people in this country, if you don't have papers, you are going to get sent back no matter what. I felt really weird about that. My parents started asking us, "Would you want to live with your brother? Would you want to live with your aunt?" My sister and I started crying because we thought we were going to lose our parents. It was so difficult finding out that we didn't have papers. And we could be separated because of that. That day will stick in my mind my entire life.

My dad works at this factory where there are a lot of undocumented people. Immigration and Customs Enforcement (ICE) was just everywhere. He had started thinking, "What if they do get me, what's going to happen to my kids?"

I couldn't say anything. I was really angry. How am I supposed to choose where I'm supposed to live? I want to live with my parents. I want to be with them my entire life. I was angry that I had to be scared because we didn't have a number. A number makes you a person. It didn't matter that both of my parents have college degrees, that they pay taxes. Nothing mattered, nothing mattered, nothing mattered.

High school is a very tough time in your life where you are judged everywhere. If anybody found out that I didn't have papers, then, oh my goodness! If I don't keep it a secret, people will look at me differently. I would be criticized, people would make fun of me, and people will threaten me, saying things like *"la migra, la migra!"* They would start yelling that. I've seen it happen at my school. My really good best friends know. And my boyfriend knows. But if I told people, they would treat me differently. Being in high school and not having a Social Security number also limits you a lot as to what things you can do.

When I hear people say "illegal alien," I feel like they are referring to me as if I was from another planet, as if I wasn't from the same earth, the same soil that they were brought up on. I don't think a human can be "illegal." I use the word "undocumented" because due to a document you don't have the rights that everybody else has. I have the biggest hate in the world for the words "illegal alien." People don't realize that this country was formed through immigration.

There is so much unfairness in this world. The anger inside builds and builds and gives you courage. With all the unfairness and injustice in this world, you just want to do something. I'm not just going to sit here and whine about it, I'm going to go out there and do something about it.

On Ne Transige Pas avec L'Éducation

Moi aussi j'ai des rêves
On est né avec ce bien légitime
Voler plus haut que soi-même
Se chercher et se trouver
L'homme est le fils de ses rêves

L'utopie s'est arrêtée sous mon toit
Depuis que j'ai decouvert qui je suis
Un étranger ici comme ailleurs
Un étranger a moi-même
L'étrange victime d'un cercle maudit

Terre d'opportunités O espoir interdit
Tu m'as tout donné
Tu m'as tout repris
Je n'ai des valeurs que les tiennes
Pourquoi m'as-tu abandonné?

On t'habille aux couleurs de xénophobie
On compose ton cœur a la méchanceté
Pourtant depuis l'aube des temps
Tu as ouvert tes bras à tous
L'assaut du sommet du mont rêve

Libérez les pistes du savoir
L'éducation est un trésor inaliénable
L'obstruer c'est semer l'ignorance
Casser l'homme briser l'avenir
L'homme n'est rien sans l'école.

There Can Be No Compromise On Education

I too have dreams
One is born with this rightful gift
To fly higher than oneself
To search for and find oneself
Man is the son of his own dreams

Utopia came and stayed under my roof
Ever since I discovered who I am
A stranger here as elsewhere
A stranger to myself
The strange victim of a vicious circle

Land of opportunities Oh forbidden hope
You've given me everything
You've taken it all back
I have nothing but those values of yours
Why have you abandoned me?

We dress you in the colors of xenophobia
We mold your heart into wickedness
And yet since the dawn of time
You have opened your arms to all
The assault on the summit of mount dream

Free the paths to knowledge
Education is an inalienable treasure
To obstruct it is to sow ignorance
Break man destroy the future
Man is nothing without school

- Translated by Héctor M. Miramontes

Whether America wanted us or not
we became her children.

In November, 1986, three days before my second birthday, my parents entered the United States on a six-month visitor's visa with no intention of leaving. We came from England. I've never understood why they decided to come here. They weren't running from any particular hardship or poverty or persecution. What I do know is that within the first year of our arrival we were homeless and that my childhood was consumed with fear, neglect and abuse.

They admitted that it was a mistake but it wasn't one that they were willing to fix. They said going back wasn't a possibility and though the words were never spoken aloud, my parents valued their pet dog more than their own children. At the time, British law required quarantine for any animals brought in from abroad. They didn't want the dog to suffer by returning. Instead they sentenced their daughters to years of imprisonment, placating us that we'd be "just fine" once we got married.

I was only six when I learned about my undocumented, illegal status. Because of our white skin and American mannerisms and accents, my parents thought my sister and I could and would pass as natural-born US citizens, thickening the cloak that they were hiding under. They used scare tactics to ensure our silence and compliance, telling us that we could never tell anyone that we weren't born in America. They told us that we didn't belong here, that no one wanted us here and if the wrong people found out there would be a SWAT-team-like raid bursting into our house, allowing us only one suitcase and 24 hours to leave the country.

I'd have nightmares of men dressed entirely in black with guns drawn coming into my bedroom, grabbing me and ripping me away from all of the things I loved. I'd kick and bite and scream desperately trying to get free. I'd wake up in the middle of the night, covered in sweat and lay awake trying to plan what I would take with me if those men ever really did come.

I was beaten and molested for years, beginning at a young age. I never told anyone because I was convinced that neighbors, teachers and police were avenues that would lead to deportation. I wish I could place the blame solely on the one man who was responsible, and release myself and all the other men in the world from his shame and guilt, but I'm not there yet. My greatest fear is that I'll never get there. At this point my one and only key to freedom and stability is marriage, but just the idea of a romantic relationship is shadowed by my phobic avoidance of men. I think back on those childhood condolences of "just" get married and think of the impossibility of that, even for the typical person. I'm 26 years old and sometimes it feels like this burden I carry gets a little heavier with each day that slips away from me that I'm not living my life to the fullest.

When I graduated from high school in 2002, it was a bittersweet accomplishment. I was only seventeen and I felt like the half-life I was living was over. I couldn't get a job, drive, sign a lease, open a bank account, or apply for the financial aid or loans that I would need for college. I had kept my status a secret from almost everyone; I didn't know how to tap into the community of other undocumented young people. I was alone and scared and depressed. I thought often of hurting myself.

I spent months in bed, paralyzed by overwhelming hopelessness. I credit a baby named Jacob for restoring meaning to my life. A friend, who would later become like a sister, needed someone to watch him and she knew I wasn't working, although at the time she didn't know why. I gladly accepted the responsibility. He gave me a reason to get up in the morning. He gave me someone to focus on and pour my energy into. He made me laugh and gave me the ability to experience joy again. He gave me a reason and value and an idea for a business model. I began working as a nanny; it was something that I was good at and enjoyed. Today I work for numerous families, most of whom know about my status and all that matters to them is that their children love me.

Jacob is nine now and I still see him almost every day. I try my hardest to hold onto all the good things. I'm grateful for every person who has helped me on this journey. I have a big sister and friends who love me. I get to be an aunt to two amazing little boys. After seven years of paying for one class at a time at a painstakingly slow pace I'm only two credits away from getting my associate's degree. I learned very early not to take anything for granted. Yet, sometimes I feel guilty that I want so much more. I still wish for a thousand things to be different. I still ask why, a lot. I still cry about it. But mostly I think I will eventually be okay.

My parents made a bad choice and I do think there should be consequences for them. But it wasn't my choice. I think of being an undocumented child in this country and I think of babies that are left on the doorstep of a stranger's home. Maybe the parents abandoned their baby because they were selfish or maybe they left their child because they truly believed that was the only way for it to survive, but the end result is the same. The door is opened, the baby looked down upon and it is up to the person on the other side if that door will be slammed shut in disgust, or if that baby full of innocence, life and potential will be scooped up in embrace. Whether America wanted us or not we became her children.

G et in line!" they like to say without realizing that many of us were at some point in this infamous line. My family immigrated to the United States from Iran when I was just three years old. At the time my dad was accepted by a university on a student visa to get his doctoral degree. After three years he completed his studies and applied for something called Optional Practical Training (OPT), essentially allowing him to extend his stay for twelve months. During that time, he would be able to continue to work and study in the same field in which he received his PhD.

While still under the OPT program, my dad secured sponsorship from a job and applied for a change of status from OPT to an H-1B visa. The university's immigration attorney handled all of the paperwork. My parents paid the required fee and they were told that everything was set to go, or so they thought. Until this point, we still had legal status, we were still "in line." Eventually a letter came from the Immigration and Naturalization Service (INS) stating that the application was rejected because the fee that had been enclosed hadn't been for the right amount. Apparently INS had raised its fee the previous year and it was now $20 more than we were instructed by the attorney to provide.

My parents immediately hired an attorney who was independent from the university but that attorney failed to inform my parents that they only had sixty days to appeal the decision. The attorney failed to take any measures to protect our status or to inform us of what could be done. And so we lost legal status.

I now find myself in a constant state of limbo. I am currently enrolled in the Social Work program at my college, and I have always volunteered within the local community. I have been offered several jobs that I have had to unfortunately decline.

I can't see myself living anywhere else other than America. All my childhood memories are from America and it is the only home I have known. Apart from that, I also happen to be gay. If one is at all up to date on their current events, I am sure you know how unfriendly a place Iran is for anyone who happens to be LGBTQ (Lesbian, Gay, Bisexual, Trans, Queer).

Iran is one of the countries that not only punishes people for being gay, but also kills them. Mahmoud Asgari (16) and Ayaz Marhoni (18) are two teenagers who were killed for no reason other than being gay. In addition to the outright intolerance towards homosexuality, it is the view of the Iranian clerics that the cure to homosexuality is a sex-change operation. Going back to Iran is not an option for me.

The only difference I see between myself and the next American is $20, two strong cases of legal malpractice, and a piece of paper.

ACT IV

I Could Not Be Silent Any Longer

I hope everybody understands that immigrant students are not very different from their children. Think of us as your children's — your sons' and daughters' — friends. We are not aliens.

— Yo Sub, *Papers* documentary film

They call me Ibby and I am from Nigeria, the most populous African nation. I migrated to the United States during the winter season, November, 1996, and that was when I was eleven years old. My only purpose in moving to the States was because of my hearing loss. Before I would make my flight to the States, my mom and my sister were already here, migrating in 1994. My mom came up with the idea that my father should send me to her so she could seek better help for my hearing.

My first thought upon arriving was to see the SNOW! Oh yes, I know it sounds a bit crazy, but ask me how many times did I watch *Home Alone* while in Nigeria. Remember the scene where Kevin had to run up to the homeless guy just to wish him a "Merry Christmas" and to share his friendship bond by giving him a turtle dove? You see the snow, right? That's what got me so excited. Unfortunately, upon my arrival there was no snow. It was just a bitter cold.

My doctors could not do anything about my hearing but suggested I start using hearing aids inserted in both ears. Another option they suggested was for me to get a cochlear implant. To be honest, I preferred the hearing aids over the cochlear implant because I felt that for me to be deaf is just part of my life's destination. You can't cheat life by trying too hard to make a U-turn just because you missed something. Whatever happens in life, you learn to appreciate it for this is part of your fate. I just appreciate who I am and the disability of not hearing.

I only wish I had the intellect of a grown man when eleven years old. Had I known of my trouble, I would not have hesitated to solve the issue. I only found out my problem later when applying to college and they requested my Social Security number. That was when I realized I did not have one and immediately made a trip, with the help of my sign language interpreter, to the Social Security office. Unfortunately, I was denied one upon my request. I was informed that I had overstayed my visa and I needed to take the matter to the Immigration office. I met with an immigration lawyer and they explained everything to me. Their explanation did not help but got me quite upset. What really upset me was the fact that they could not help me since I was eighteen years old and everything had become all my responsibility. Even though I could accept the fact that everything was now my responsibility, allowing me to battle my case with the immigration judge at the court was deemed "risky" by one of my lawyers.

My teacher had heart and understood my situation. She was a true American. She decided to write a letter in regards to my situation to one congressman. My case was ignored. We didn't lose, it's just that nobody in the government workforce was willing to take up my fight. All I can do is thank them for not calling ICE (Immigration and Customs Enforcement) on me, for I was clueless as to who ICE was and what their tasks were.

Today, I am 25 years old and still living in the States. I have grown up a gentleman and have learned a lot here, which I think if I still lived in Nigeria, I would never have learned and would never be who I am today. My quest to be an Art Therapist has made me develop the ability to withstand the things I could not. It also helps me to be patient with my situation as undocumented.

As a deaf person, I figured Art Therapy could enable the people in the deaf community to build confidence in themselves when encountering the hearing community. It is no secret that many people in the deaf community feel the hatred from the hearing community. With those feelings, it makes them become subordinate. With the use of Art Therapy, they may be able to understand their inner feelings and brush off those critical assumptions by the hearing community. Many deaf people feel afraid to use their voices when in the real world. I want them to go out and be able to use their voices more often. The thought of someone laughing or mimicking them prevents them from using their voice. I understand the beauty of being deaf and its community, but this does not mean we have to remain silent or mute and allow the stereotyping to continue to conquer us.

After trying to request internships where I can continue my focus in Art Therapy, I have been denied the opportunity due to my immigration status. Now I can only wait for the DREAM Act to pass so I can grab the opportunity to achieve my goals, nationwide and globally.

I am originally from Jakarta, Indonesia. I am an undocumented student.

The period leading up to my family's immigration was a bleak time in Indonesian history. It was a time of great economic and political unrest. Riots and looting were commonplace. The country was in an economic crisis and the prices of daily necessities spiked greatly. Many people were jobless, including my parents.

The broken storefront windows, the demonstrations and the burning car tires created a brand new playground in my overactive mind. Little did I know that student demonstrators were being gunned down by the army and that minorities were being persecuted. People were suffering greatly.

When my dad left for the United States to prepare "the way" for the rest of us, he promised us a trip to Disneyland and a better life. Little did I know he had to work long hours in bone-breaking jobs as a day laborer.

When our family arrived in the US, my little sister was four, my little brother was seven, I was eleven, and my big sister was thirteen. We came here with tourist visas, but quickly applied for asylum status after we arrived. We applied on the basis of religious persecution.

We were a Christian family in a Muslim majority. During that time there were a lot of cases of church lootings and anti-Christian violence. We thought we had a good case but it turned out that it was not enough. We never had "direct experience with violence or persecution," nor did we have "imminent life-threatening danger upon returning." After several years of waiting and trying to appeal the case, it failed and we lost our temporary status.

During that struggle, I was in high school and I was trying to do the best I could. But every time I saw my parents' disappointed faces I was pretty disheartened. I mean, they worked so hard for us and they tried their best to live here "legally." I thought we were treated unfairly by the immigration system. I grew more and more disillusioned with everything around me.

Luckily, around this time I got involved with community organizing. I realized that other members of the community, regardless of documents, suffer from the same systemic injustice. I learned about the world as it is now, and the world as I want it to be, as it ought to be. As members of the community, we all possess the political power to stand against injustice for the betterment of our communities and our lives. This was a novel idea for me as an undocumented youth who is not able to vote.

This brought me back not only the power to dream and imagine, but also the power to take pride in my community and in my country. It gave me great strength knowing that people are with me in my struggles and knowing that the struggles of all marginalized people in the US are my struggles as well. I'm learning to not take anything for granted and to keep on fighting for the rights of youth like me and for every poor and oppressed minority in my country, the United States.

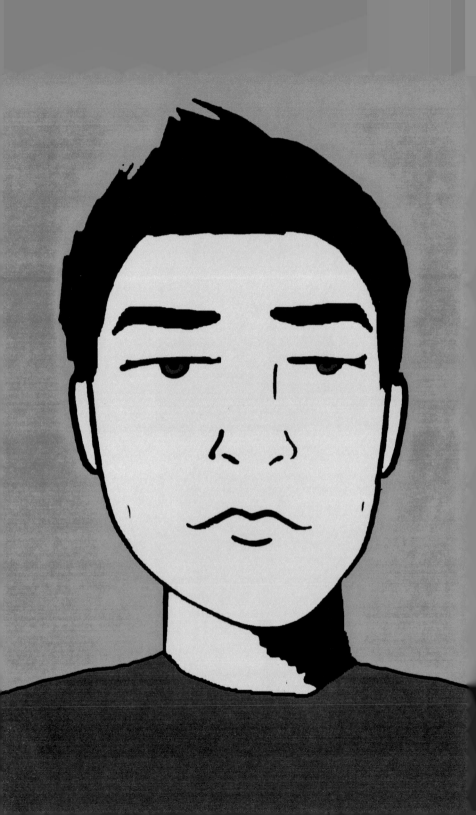

I grew up in the San Francisco Bay Area. Just like many other American kids, I went to public school, spoke English, joined student government, participated in sports, and took Advanced Placement (AP) classes. Most importantly, I was motivated to go to college. However, my dreams were completely shattered when I learned that my tourist visa had expired and I was living here without proper documentation. At the age of seventeen, I first found out about my status and I never thought that I would be one of an estimated 11.5 million undocumented immigrants in this country.

Although I am 21 years old, I feel like I am a little kid because I cannot do certain things that my American citizen friends can do. For example, I cannot freely travel around, study abroad or obtain a driver's license. These limitations caused me a lot of jealously towards my citizen friends.

When I first learned about my immigration status, I was ashamed of who I was. I didn't want to reveal my status to anyone because I was too embarrassed by the fact that I cannot do certain things and was afraid of being deported. As a result, I remained in silence and stayed in a closet for a very long time. However, I realized that hiding my status did not help me fix my situation at all. Instead, I became more frustrated and upset about my limitations due to lack of documentation. At one point, I seriously thought of committing suicide.

Being an Asian undocumented student, it was extremely challenging to "come out" because there aren't many support systems within our own community. Instead, there's a lot of cultural stigma and social discrimination against undocumented immigrants. They tend to look down upon undocumented immigrants and treat us like inferior beings.

However, as I was looking at my mother, working twelve hours a day, seven days a week, sacrificing her time and energy to support my education, I knew I couldn't just give up. Because of her willingness to sacrifice for my future, I decided to focus on school and devote my time to research on AB 540 (a California state law that provides in-state tuition for California high school graduates, including undocumented students) and the DREAM Act and to figure out ways to fix my immigration status.

While I was researching, I found dozens of articles and testimonies of other undocumented students. Of those many courageous students, Tam Tran's story stood out the most because she was the only Asian undocumented student that I had read at that time. With her courage and speaking on behalf of other undocumented students, I was inspired and motivated to come out and share my testimony as well.

In early January, 2011, I decided to publicly "come out" and speak to the Korean-American media. I could not be silent any longer and it was a moment for me to go public and speak on behalf of the undocumented community at large.

At first, my mother was hesitant about my decision of going public in the Korean-American press. Just like many other undocumented parents, my mother was concerned about facing deportation. But eventually my mother allowed me to come out in the Korean press. Once she read dozens of articles about my story, she was very proud.

I am a senior at UC Berkeley, studying political science. After I graduate from Berkeley, I hope to take one or two years off from school and work at a non-profit organization to help the immigrant community at large. Eventually, I want to go back to school and study law and ultimately I want to become an immigration lawyer.

I consider myself an American and America will always be my home. I want to let young people know that they are not alone in this struggle.

I am an undocumented student who graduated as the valedictorian of my high school. Currently, I am a sophomore studying Mechanical Engineering at a private university, where the tuition is extremely high. I have to come up with this money all on my own with no help of government financial help. I can't work and it frustrates me everyday. I love this country and I want to contribute to our economy but unfortunately I am an undocumented immigrant. I believe that this country was founded by people from all nations, colors and races. Just because it has been more than 200 years doesn't mean that the immigration gates should be closed! We need to fight for our rights.

I was captain of the track and
cross country teams, editor of
the high school paper, in the
Honor Society, yet going to
college was almost impossible.

As a former undocumented student I know the struggles undocumented people go through. I was brought to the United States from Mexico when I was three and to be honest, I really didn't know I was undocumented until I was a junior in high school. That's when it hit me. I was the captain of the track and cross country teams, editor of the high school paper, in the Honor Society, yet going to college was almost impossible. At the time, tuition for "non-residents" like me was over ten times what everyone else was paying. Luckily private scholarships paid for all my years of college.

When I graduated from college I was named "Outstanding Graduating Senior" for my department: Journalism. Imagine: an "illegal alien" being called "outstanding!" (By the way, I hate the term "illegal alien.") Unfortunately, I had a nice degree without a Social Security number to back it up. I ended up going to graduate school and during the last year there I was given residency: after waiting for 21 years! I cannot explain how much my life has changed. I went from helping my mom clean houses to being a producer in television. What papers can do!

ACT V

Setting an Upside-Down World Right-Side Up

Being part of this cause, fighting for it, being an activist, makes me part of something and when you're part of something you feel like you belong. You feel you are part of something that's special and you're making a change and you're just making your community better.

— Jorge, *Papers* documentary film

I remember watching my parents
work day and night, stooping down
to people, seeing my dad cry for the
first time. I have never seen them
this vulnerable in my life.

My name is Jamie and I am a college sophomore majoring in International Relations and Economics at Fullerton College. My parents decided to emigrate from South Korea to the United States ten years ago, due to the financial damage that the International Monetary Fund Bankruptcy caused in 1997. They believed that America would provide a better future and opportunities for my sister and me and our family would essentially have a fresh start at life.

Just like any other American story, our family started from scratch. I remember watching my parents work day and night, stooping down to people, seeing my dad cry for the first time. I have never seen them this vulnerable in my life. So I turned to education as my only escape from poverty. For the next few years, I worked hard to learn English. I got involved with the International Baccalaureate program, Honors and Advanced Placement (AP) classes and varsity tennis. I served as the president of my high school's speech and debate team and the environmental awareness club. I worked hard because I wanted to be somebody and have the opportunity to experience the world. American society tells us that if you work hard you will be able to obtain your American Dream. But that wasn't the case. Despite all the qualified grades and extracurricular activities and the passion I had for higher education, I viewed even obtaining a vocational degree as a challenge because of the status that I had no choice in making.

When I was nine, the thought of legal immigration and the types of visas didn't cross my mind. I just did what I was told. I don't think my parents had any idea that 9/11 would alter our (US) immigration policy and put us in the situation that we are in right now. When I first found out, I thought, "Okay, this is a land of immigrants." I was sure there would be some type of policy that would help these large groups of students. I looked up how to get naturalized by military service or any type of program I could get my hands on but it was just a "Catch-22" chain of impossibility.

During my junior and senior years of high school, I fell into depression. I felt confused, angry and sad. I did everything to the best of my ability to attempt to receive the type of education and experience I wanted for myself. But I couldn't. I no longer felt like I could relate to my peers and even felt isolated at times in the

DREAM Act movement that was heavily dominated by Latinos. Unfortunately, people often believe that "undocumentation" is a small faction issue that only affects Latinos, but it can happen to anyone from any country who chooses to come to the United States. They can't gain an education, access to civil rights or even a simple thing such as nutrition. Even regular immigrants can get cut out by lawyers misfiling their papers.

I dream one day to be part of the US Air Force and State Department and ultimately become the human rights director for the United Nations. I want to give back to this country that has given so many opportunities to me. For a long time, when I was young, I believed that living in America meant being whoever you wanted to be, despite your gender, race, social class or sexual orientation. If you aspired to be someone and worked hard at it, it was possible. That thought has deteriorated over the years.

Today I give "AB 540 Workshops" to students in Orange County, mostly Korean students and anyone else who wants to listen. These workshops are about the AB 540 tuition exemption program that is accessible in California, private scholarships, and other basic survival skills that young people may find useful as undocumented students wanting to continue higher education. I always wished that I had somebody, especially a fellow Asian DREAMer, telling me that it was still possible to go on to college and show me the resources that may have helped me in the future. That is why I am stepping out to help others who are finding themselves in the same situation that I am in. The sooner they receive support and acceptance, the more motivated these DREAMers will be to fight for their education.

My fellow DREAMers are the most passionate, intelligent, and motivated people I have ever met in my life. They are the reason why I no longer live in fear and in shame. They are the reason why I believe that I am going to accomplish everything I aspire to achieve in the future. I am going to do everything I can to fight for my and our future. It is not just a Latino issue, it's a universal fight for equal education. The longer we hold off the DREAM Act, the longer the DREAMer's future is on hold.

There are people living here who are gay and undocumented and they feel like they have to hide. I think you just have to be open and say who you are. You're always going to be taking a risk. I'm gay and I'm undocumented.

Being gay and undocumented is a little harder because you face discrimination for both things, you get judged for both things. Sometimes my own people, the Latino community, can be closed-minded about gay people. When I'm in the gay, lesbian, bisexual, transgender community, I feel we're a big family who will support each other. I like that. I feel very comfortable and it gives me courage.

I came out to my family because I didn't want to live a double life, being one person at home and another person with my friends. I'm not going to live in the closet. I'm going to be me. I want to be courageous. There are similarities between coming out as undocumented and coming out as being gay. You fear that people will reject you and that your friends might look at you weird or feel like you lied to them. You don't know how they're going to react.

When I came out as undocumented to my friends I felt like I didn't have to hide anymore and they respected me. Before I came out, I was more quiet and I didn't say what I thought, but now I speak my mind and tell people what I think and believe.

I went to my first Gay Pride parade this year in the city and I felt really happy. It felt like we were a big family, that we supported each other, that we have each other's backs and we were Asian, African American, Latino, Anglo, undocumented and documented. I felt love in my community. That's what we need more in the straight and immigrant communities: to love and support each other more. I think the straight and immigrant communities could learn from the Lesbian, Gay, Bisexual, Trans, Queer (LGBTQ) community.

We're living in the 21st century; we have stop caring so much what people think. People are always going to talk about you. But I'm not going to live a life for them, trying to make them happy when I'm miserable. The people who are going to love you are going to love you for who you are.

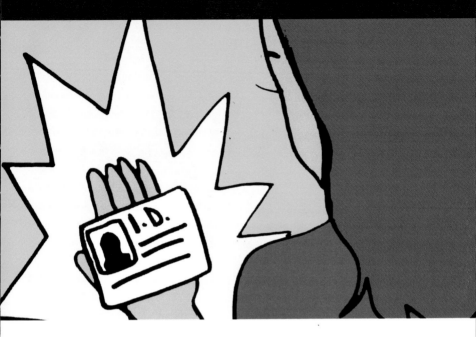

You can't tell by looking at me that up until two months ago, I was an undocumented immigrant. I have lived in California for 28 years of my life. My family came here on a tourist visa and over-stayed. My grandfather was a US citizen and fought in WWII and even received bronze stars for his involvement.

My grandfather had petitioned for legal status for our family. But he passed away and the petition died with him until it was finally reinstated. In waiting I had reached the age of eighteen, then 21, and was no longer on the petition. My parents divorced and both remarried US citizens and my brother was born here. So everyone was fine except for me.

My father petitioned for me in 2001, but that was a waiting game too. I never took the short road (fake marriage) and always remained under the radar. I was able to go to college and able to find work. I met the man who I wanted to spend the rest of my life with (legitimately). We have a son who is eight months old. It's funny, a few weeks ago I received my California ID in the mail. I kept staring at it for what seemed like hours, astonished to finally have an ID in my hands. It feels like the whole world is open to me now.

Our experiences as queer youth place us on paths of great self-discovery, paths of overcoming adversity, of setting what feels like upside-down worlds right-side up again.

This story begins in a seaside town in the state of Michoacan in México. I'm the daughter of an amazing woman who had me at a very young age. It was 1985, my mother was sixteen with only an eighth grade education and with many dreams left to be fulfilled, when I was born. From then on, my mother and I shared our struggles. She was a single mother and had been kicked out of her house because of, well, me.

As many other women in poorer areas of México do, she began doing odd jobs: running a sandwich stand, house-cleaning, sewing needle-point pillowcases, making jello and meals to sell to military stationed nearby, selling candies. She did whatever was needed to make ends meet.

I had had little contact with my father who had left my mother soon after she had gotten pregnant, but in 1992, he made contact with my mother again. It was then, according to the story *mi mamá* tells me, that he expressed that he wanted us to be together again. He had been in the United States for a few years and wanted us to join him. By then my mother was 24 and knew she wanted a better life for me, something she would not be able to give me in México as a single mother. This began our journey and story in the United States.

I remember my first holiday in the US. It was Halloween and I was seven years old. I'd never seen so many kids and I never knew you could get free candy just for wearing something silly. You can imagine, I was thrilled. Soon after arriving I began school here and excelled at it. I graduated with honors from high school but faced an uncertain future. I didn't know if I would attend college or how I would afford it. I thought my hopes and dreams ended with graduation. It was bittersweet.

However, I managed to overcome the obstacles and graduated from a two-year college in 2006. Soon after, I began my activist journey. It was 2007 when I first attended an action – the DREAM Graduation in Washington, DC – and I became hooked. For the first time in my life, I met a large group of people who shared a similar narrative as I did. They knew my struggles, they shared my anguish, frustration and anger at the system that oppressed us. They also shared my hunger for justice. This was also the year I came out as LGBT (Lesbian, Gay, Bisexual, Trans).

I knew we existed. We, the UndocuQueer. We'd shared our stories, we'd bonded over loves lost, coming out to our loved ones, our educational struggles, the broken immigration system and the need for a place where we fit. Yet our stories weren't out there. We existed, mostly, in silence.

By 2010, I was very active in DREAM Act organizing, had been to Washington, DC multiple times and had my feet relatively well planted in the politics of Capitol Hill. Up until this point, my queer life and my undocumented life hadn't really intermingled outside of myself. Within both movements, there was little room for me to be my true self. I was either undocumented or queer; never both. I first came out as undocumented to a room full of unknown people who had no idea what that meant or how that affected me personally. It was both extremely scary and amazingly liberating.

Like worlds colliding, a month after that I was sitting in a meeting with immigrant youth from across the country discussing and planning what would be known as "Coming Out of the Shadows Day": a day where the immigrant youth movement, led by many queer youth, would borrow what we'd learned from our sisters and brothers in the LGBT struggle and follow Harvey Milk's example of "coming out." It was simple but so life-changing; revolutionary at its core.

Some ask, why is it that so many immigrant youth leaders happen to be queer? What I do know is that our stories and our experiences as queer youth place us on paths of great self-discovery, paths of overcoming adversity, of setting what feels like upside-down worlds right-side up again, of discovering one's true self and loving what one sees. It's a path of learning and lending a hand to those that follow because we know what it's like to be in their shoes. We know it's hard, we know it hurts but we also know we're strong, beautiful human beings with the ability to make change, both within ourselves and outside of ourselves. I believe those paths, once travelled, leave us with stories unlike anyone else's.

The same holds true for the undocumented. Like Rigoberta Menchú, we too are "privileged witnesses of an oppressive system." We too are stubbornly determined to break the silence. We have broken it. We will continue to break it. We refuse to let anyone forget. I refuse to let anyone forget. We are undocumented and unafraid. Queer and unashamed.

I knew we were leaving our friends, family and country. I was
ready and knew that I was not going to be scared since my
habuelitos told me I was a warrior and our ancestors were war-
riors. I don't remember much until the day I was on the other side
of that fence.

My parents had sold their property in Mexico, left their family,
risked their lives and their children's lives to pursue not just an
"American Dream" but their dignity and pride as parents. The first
three years of my life in the US were depressing, frustrating, and
worst of all, I didn't know if my parents had received their dignity
back since my dad had lost his job a couple of months after we
arrived.

If you were to ask me what were the best years of my life I
would answer my high school years in the United States and my
elementary years in Mexico. Continuing to adapt to my new home
country, but not forgetting my country of birth and culture. Still

playing soccer but loving football. From eating fast food to eating at restaurants. From family being first to friends being my priority. From listening to Spanish music to loving hip-hop. From dancing to folkloric Mexican music to breakdancing. From being an honor student to "I'm trying my best." From being happy sometimes to being sad at times. From hanging out with trouble-makers to hanging out with football stars and cheerleaders. From getting respect from my Latino friends to them seeing me as a traitor, from not fitting in with the white kids but assimilating to my black friends.

I graduated from high school with the class of 2004. I was the first in my family to graduate. My parents were really happy for me and with themselves since they had sacrificed a lot to see us graduate from high school with the hope of pursuing college.

Some years later, I received great news. I found out I was going to be a dad and start my own family. I was happy and excited. However, I still felt scared since I was still undocumented and now I had to protect and support another human being. I was not just a DREAMer, but now a DREAMer parent. I started thinking back to the words of wisdom of my grandparents and the sacrifices my parents, family and ancestors made to give us a better life. That motivated me to keep on fighting for my own family and my little one.

I was frustrated about what was going on in our communities and all these anti-immigrant laws being voted on in the state legislatures. Many times I couldn't sleep and couldn't focus at work. I couldn't focus on my family and was feeling unhappy. I kept wondering why I was feeling this way. I mean, I had supportive parents, I was healthy, I had accomplished some of my goals both in my life and my career, my partner was expecting a healthy baby.

I was still living in fear and did not understand what it meant to be undocumented and proud of it. I started to get more and more involved with a group of youth, both documented and undocumented. I felt a belonging despite our age differences, our different cultures, ethnicities, languages and immigration status.

Finally, it seemed that our DREAMs were coming true. The DREAM Act was getting all this national attention. People started to rally and lobby, school districts started to be supportive of such a bill, most senators started to be supportive, but I asked myself if it was true. Did it even have a chance?

In December of 2010 we found out that the DREAM Act was going to be introduced as a stand-alone bill. Was this true? Did it have a chance? Is it politics that they are talking about? Should I get excited? Should I care? Should I fight for it? How? I can't vote. Do we have the votes to pass? What is the first thing I'm going to do if it passes? What is the process once it passes? Finally I would be able to attend college and then continue with my DREAMs, finally I would be accepted into American society, finally I would feel part of this country. I was connected with a group of youth and started to mobilize and get active, for the first time I was active politically, I was calling senators to support the DREAM Act. I started to use social media to communicate with other undocumented youth and stay updated with the DREAM Act. Everything seemed that it was in our favor and we had this, at least that was what I wanted to believe, finally we were going to be living without fear.

The week of the vote had come and I was running on few hours of sleep but it was all worth it. The day had come, all that we had worked for was going to pay off, my DREAMs were in the hands of some senators, I was watching it on the internet, then woke up all my family and called friends and relatives. I turned on the TV and the show had begin, it was the moment of truth, the moment had begun for senators to choose our future, my parents' dignity was going to be back, the fear was going to be gone, my daughter was not going to be ashamed of her dad, I was going to be able to see other places I could not go to due to my immigration status, my friends were also going to continue their DREAMs, my little brother and sister would benefit and continue their DREAMs. The moment was here, the vote started, I was really nervous and wanted to throw up. Minutes later we saw the total number of votes. It didn't pass. I wanted to cry but decided to just move on and treat the day like any other.

After the vote I felt really outraged and wanted to scream really loud! At that moment I decided to do my best to not give up and continue to work hard and bring back the DREAM Act and Immigration Reform. I promised that we were going to be heard loud and no longer was I going to hide in the shadows. I was going to work really hard so other undocumented youth would not have to go through what I went through. After the vote it became about other people, not about me. I promise I will walk till my feet get blisters, write till my fingertips get worn from writing, work till my eyes close because of fatigue.

This new chapter of my life is dedicated to all those DREAMers who have sacrificed so much so that we don't have to feel that a piece of paper makes us human. This chapter of my life I have decided to no longer be afraid, to not be ashamed, and to wear my identity with pride and my head held high.

resh out of journalism school, I was eager to go out into the world and put my degree to work. I wanted to tell the untold stories that didn't necessarily make it to the six o'clock news. Growing up as a gay undocumented Latino in the United States, I rarely read stories about people like myself. Curious to know how other undocumented college graduates were using their degrees, I pitched a story idea to a news website based in New York. While working on that story, I met Tony. He nearly brought me to tears as he told me a story that involved Immigration and Customs Enforcement (ICE) raiding his house and some agents making fun of his effeminate behavior.

As a gay man myself, I felt like this was something our immigrant and queer community should know about so I decided to investigate. I wanted to get ICE's side of the story so I tried to give them a call. But when I called the detention center that Tony had been taken to, I panicked and quickly hung up. What if they asked me for my papers? What if they investigated me? What if they went after my family? I had this degree in journalism that I couldn't use because I was too afraid of the possibility of ending up in Tony's shoes.

Disappointed with myself for not having the guts to continue with the story, I decided to stop writing and go back to my sketch pad. It's strange how all this pent up anger began to fuel my creative juices. Using the stories of my close undocumented friends and my own experiences, I created a comic strip called *Liberty For All* about a twenty-something undocumented college graduate working at a dead-end job. Through *Liberty* I re-created scenarios familiar to a lot of us. Getting these stories out there empowered me in a way I didn't think was possible. I was managing to use my degree in a very creative way.

In 2010, as photographs of undocumented college students getting arrested during acts of civil disobedience began to show up on my Facebook News Feed, I knew I just had to document what was happening. Thanks to online media and social networking, my drawings began to go viral. They truly resonated with students across the nation who were being labeled, by some, as criminals. Students began to send me messages thanking me for posting the illustrations. But it was them I was thankful for. These brave students were coming out of the shadows and standing up for what is right. I was just very lucky to be able to draw them.

In my encounters with undocumented artists, poets and writers, I can see their pain. I can sense their struggle. No one but ourselves can truly capture our stories on paper or images on canvas. Others are only just beginning to realize the reality in which we live. While working on the images for this book, I was working as a line cook at a popular Mexican restaurant chain. There were many late nights when I'd arrive at my parents' home and make myself read some of these stories. While I was reading them, there was a spark inside of me that moved me to create no matter how tired I was. I could see myself in many of these stories. As I read them, there was a scene playing inside of my head that was aching to get out.

I've made drawings of hundreds of undocumented immigrant youth. I've lost count of how many. When someone asks me why I make these illustrations, I don't know how to explain this urge to document our struggle. For years, reporters and academics have gotten paid to research and explain our struggle to others. But I don't know that they've gotten the whole story right. Nobody but us can tell what is like to be undocumented.

I have met only a few of the people in this collection of stories. For the most part, I don't know what they actually look like. Sometimes I had physical descriptions to go by but mostly I used my instinct. In this age of instant photo sharing, I purposely didn't want to see photographs because I wanted to focus on their stories. I don't have an explanation for this; it just worked better. I truly hope to one day meet each one of the people I drew in this book.

The process of illustrating this book was one more reminder of how much the DREAM Act or Comprehensive Immigration Reform is needed in this country. Living with fear is probably one of the worst feelings any human being can experience. Bringing together stories like these and being able to publish them for others to read is a step in the right direction of justice. My name is Julio Salgado. I am queer, undocumented, unafraid and I exist.

ACKNOWLEDGMENTS

We would like to express our gratitude to all the writers who submitted their stories. Thank you for your generosity and courage.

We are grateful to our readers Thalia Zepatos and Randy Chambers for reviewing the manuscript. Their advice was invaluable. Any mistakes are our own. Thanks to Héctor M. Miramontes for the translation of Khadim's poem from French and Jorge's story from Spanish.

We would like to thank Meredith Blankinship for her enthusiasm, LynnAnn Klotz for legal advice and moral support and the Winning Mark agency for moral and financial support.

Many thanks to Abigail Marble for graphic design and layout, to Travis Omlid of TO Designs for website design and to our printer Morel Ink of Portland, Oregon.

We are deeply grateful to DreamActivist.org. They were a pioneer in collecting immigrant youth stories to build the movement and change hearts and minds. Five stories from this collection originally appeared on the DreamActivist.org website: those written by Dan, Alejandra, Cyndi, Mohammad and Hans.

We would like to offer our gratitude to all the interviewees, volunteers, donors and crew members who helped bring the documentary film *Papers: Stories of Undocumented Youth* to life. We would especially like to acknowledge Jose Luis Juarez-Perez, a founding member of *El Grupo Juvenil*, the *Papers* Youth Crew. Special thanks to *Papers* crew members Andre Nakazawa, Dunetchka Otero-Serrano, Carol Auger, Aeryca Steinbauer, Corrinne Theodoru and Adrian H. Molina.

Most of all we would like to express our profound thanks to the five youth featured in the documentary film *Papers*: Simone, Juan Carlos, Jorge, Monica and Yo Sub. By telling your stories you encouraged thousands of others to do the same.

There is no one undocumented experience. *Papers* weaves together narratives of undocumented youth who come from different countries and backgrounds. Some of our parents crossed the border without authorization, some of us came here legally and overstayed visas, some of us were escaping persecution while some came seeking more prosperity. We are from all over the world. But somewhere in all our stories there is a common thread: there is an act of love. And that is the bridge between all our differences.

> — Prerna Lal, Undocumented and Unafraid

Undocumented youth are the leaders of a cultural transformation that is sweeping the country, making huge gains for the immigrant rights movement. Unapologetic and unafraid, they are writing their own history, establishing new rules in the game and setting an example for all of us. As an artist and cultural organizer, I see the vital importance of documenting these stories through writing, poetry and art. This book illuminates the complexity of what it means to be young and undocumented today.

> — Favianna Rodriguez, artist and co-editor of *Reproduce & Revolt*

We tell stories not simply to express ourselves but to connect with each other. And that is precisely what this collection of stories accomplishes—they connect the stories of these courageous, inspiring, young undocumented Americans to the evolving story of our country which is being remade right in front of our eyes. In the dawn of the 21st century, undocumented youth are a living testament to what is enduring about the American spirit.

> — Jose Antonio Vargas, award-winning journalist and founder of Define American